DENGIE

the life and the land

by

Kevin Bruce

Published by the Essex Record Office
in collaboration with
the Burnham and District Local History and Amenity Society

Essex Record Office Publication No. 82
ISBN 0 900360 58 5

1981

The Essex Coast, while it shared many of its crafts, skills and rural activities with the rest of the County, had, across the centuries, a way of life that was peculiarly its own. This collection of photographs helps to illustrate the similarities and differences found in just one of the coastal Hundreds.

The eastern end of The Dengie Hundred is really a peninsula jutting into the North Sea. The wide Blackwater Estuary leading up to Maldon forms the northern boundary, with the narrower Crouch reaching inland as far as Battlesbridge in the south. Its seaboard contains over 11,000 acres of reclaimed marshes, making it a truly man-made landscape. The struggle to win this land, farm it, and keep it, has moulded the Dengie character and produced the crafts of the sea-waller, marshman, wild-fowler and decoyman. The sea provided the main links with the markets and supplies, as well as giving access to crops of shellfish and wildfowl.

The larger villages along this seaboard follow a belt of sand and gravel which stretches from Bradwell south-westwards to Burnham. Before reclamation began, the village centres were all a short haul from tidal creeks. Stone for its churches and, much later, Scandinavian timber for its traditional weatherboarded cottages all came by this means.

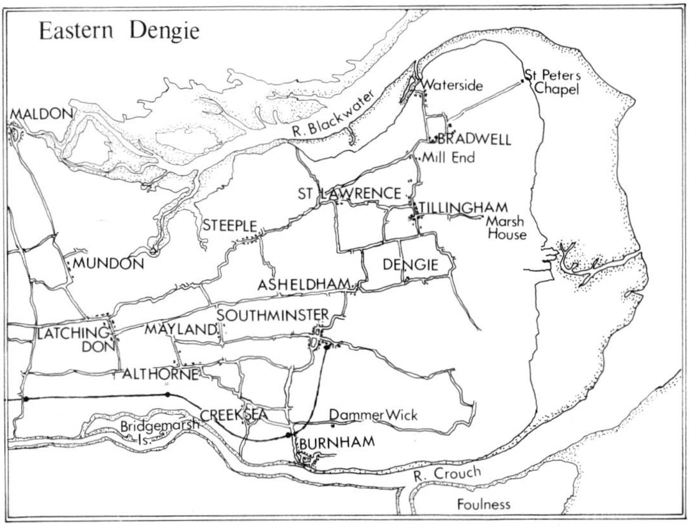
Eastern Dengie
MALDON
R. Blackwater
Waterside
St Peters
Chapel
BRADWELL
Mill End
ST LAWRENCE
TILLINGHAM
Marsh
House
STEEPLE
MUNDON
DENGIE
ASHELDHAM
SOUTHMINSTER
LATCHING
DON
MAYLAND
ALTHORNE
CREEKSEA
Dammer Wick
Bridgemarsh
Is.
BURNHAM
R. Crouch
Foulness

Burnham: a town takes shape

Burnham, the largest town in Dengie, has two centres. The Quay long ago eclipsed in importance the area around the church, with its nearby Romano-British settlement. Today, ironically, modern development is reversing this movement.

The part of the Quay by Shore Road (below) was the first firm landing-place to be reached by ships coming up the Crouch, anciently known as Burnham River. As the town grew, the Quay extended to cope with increasing traffic, taking in the marshy land on either side, allowing the reclamation of the marshes and the advance of the town down to the water's edge.

The great width of the High Street suggests a planned medieval form allowing ample space for a thriving market area. The satisfying mix of architectural styles, built up over the centuries, many masking older timber-framed buildings, has earned modern recognition as a Conservation Area.

It was the Victorians who gave the High Street its two dominant buildings, each with an impact on the skyline. The Clock Tower (top right), now the most noted landmark, dates only from 1877, erected by public subscription, in front of St Mary's School, to the memory of Laban Sweeting, prominent citizen and oyster merchant. And it was on the income from the oyster trade that the Auger family were able to build in the early Victorian period the imposing three-storied slab of Warners Hall (bottom right).

PARAFFINE
&COLZA

Victorian Burnham

During the 19th century, Burnham, unlike all its Dengie neighbours, continued to grow. From the point (above) where the curving High Street almost touches the Quay and where now stands the War Memorial, the town gradually spread back up the hill towards its ancient foundation. The old Congregational Church, seen on the right of the picture, was burnt down in 1946. Not far around the corner still stands the Baptist Church, a reminder that Burnham was one of the earliest centres of 'Anabaptism'.

The 'New Town' (top right), opposite the open fields and grounds of Hill House, was at first separate from the Quay area. The rows of terraced houses accommodated the families for whom the coastal trade, oyster fishing, yachting and the associated crafts and commerce gave employment.

At the turn of the century it was the bridge over the railway (bottom right) opened in 1889, which marked the outer limit of the built-up area. Beyond there still stretched open fields.

HILL STORES

Southminster

Southminster grew up around an early Saxon church, its name distinguishing it from St Cedd's foundation, the northern 'minster' of St Peter's Chapel in Bradwell. Once the property of the Bishops of London, later of St Osyth's Priory, and then of Charter House, Southminster became the principal village in the Hundred. Its weekly market served all the villages and it was here that the railway terminated and the new police station and county court were built in 1901.

Traditional crosswing medieval houses appear to have been a feature of the village scene before the ravages of the 20th century. At the church end of North Street stood a fine example until repeated damage by vehicles prompted the demolition of the end wing (centre building, above). Opposite, and a little further down Station Road, stood the Manor House destroyed by a bomb in the last war. The bomb drastically altered the character of Southminster. North Street (below), a busy shopping area, was devastated leaving the High Street (bottom left) to take on the role of village shopping centre.

Tillingham

Tillingham, with its preponderance of white weather-boarded houses, is today classified as an 'Outstanding Conservation Area'. The Dean and Chapter of St Paul's have been the lords of the manor since 610 A.D. They still own Tillingham Hall Farm, ensuring the village a place in the Guinness Book of Records for length of land tenure.

The Square (above) is an unusual feature for this area. On the wall of the building near the Church can be seen the sign of The Cock which, in 1902, fell victim to a local wave of temperance. A petition from the villagers against the number of local public houses resulted in its closure and conversion to a new form of public service point as a Doctor's surgery. The Old Swan (bottom right) survived. Outside its door stands the water cart which, in dry summers, when the public pumps ran dry, would deliver water from a pump in Brook Road.

The coastguards were stationed at a lonely outpost at Grange Farm from where they guarded ten miles of seawall and the creeks and marshes. They were frequent visitors with their donkey cart at the Post Office (top right), one of the first to have the telegraph installed, in order to meet the coastguard's needs.

TILLINGHAM
POSTOFFICE
A.T.PLUCK

Bradwell-on-Sea

Unlike Southminster and Tillingham where single manors within the parish gave rise to concentrated areas of housing at the centre, Bradwell originally contained several large manors, each with its associated settlement. The result is a very scattered community, with three main centres – each, in later years, with its own public house. The Queen's Head (top left) served the Mill End area with its mill, gravel pits, smithy, builder's yard, and earlier, a brickfield. The cottages on the left were demolished to cater for 'highway improvements'.

The Green Man (bottom left) at the Waterside has long been a focus for seafarers. Bradwell Creek, because of the protection of Pewit Island and its closeness to the sea, formed a significant port for the Dengie Hundred. At the turn of the century the Parker family had about twenty sailing barges working from here. It was also a coastguard station but few fishermen operated from here.

The village centre (below) clusters around the Church. The brick-fronted timber houses and tall walls give it an enclosed feeling. The King's Head has always been the social centre of the village with many groups using it as a meeting place.

The character with the stick is Mr. Verlander. He was of Dutch descent and his family may well have been involved with earlier sea defences. On the left of the group is the young Walter Linnett, the wildfowler. The tilt-covered wagon appears to be delivering hardware and goods to the local shops.

Bradwell High Street.

Church and land

Church and landscape are intimately—and economically—connected in Dengie. It was its usefulness as a farm building which probably saved St Peter's Chapel at Bradwell (top left) from decay or destruction. Originally a Saxon monastery, it became in turn parish church, chapel of ease and, for 300 years, a barn, finally being reconsecrated for worship in 1922.

Built in the gateway of the Roman coastal fort of Othona, it has witnessed every change of the character and scenery of the marshland. Those marshes to the south were gradually reclaimed by medieval farmers to provide safer pasturage for the large flocks of sheep which were the principal husbandry up to the 17th century. They provided not only meat and wool; the ewes gave milk from which came the huge cheeses known throughout Europe.

St Mary's Burnham (bottom left) owes much of its magnificence to local 16th-century prosperity based on the trade in wool and cheese.

These sheep (above) are being dipped in the very shadow of St Peter's Chapel, in the hollow between the wall of the Roman Fort and the garden of the wildfowler Walter Linnett. The Anglian Water Authority's new-style sea walls along the Dengie coast have resulted in the return of the sheep, though nowadays their prime function is to keep the larger areas of grass cropped to save the cost of mowing.

The horses of Dengie

New technology, introduced by the Dutch after 1600, hastened the reclamation of larger areas of sea-washed saltings to produce level, rectangular fields. It still required a large workforce—both of men and horses—to carry out all the work at farms like Marsh House, Tillingham (left and below), but the level fields made it easier to use machinery.

If sheep and cattle were still essential elements in the economy, the horse was critical to the working of the farm. Horse-breeding was part of the local way of life. Each year, Mr. Pawley 'from Suffolk way' would bring his stallion (above) around the Dengie farms to sire a new generation. Later, the young colts would be rounded up for sale at the annual Southminster horse-fair.

At the end of the day's work, the horses would be led to the horsepond (right) to drink and be washed down before being fed and bedded down. Even then the horseman's day was not over, returning, as he did, in the evening to check that all was well. It was this close bond with his horses and his special (and much prized) skills which earned the horseman his valued place in the rural community.

Harvest time

Harvest time required an even larger work force. It was a time when extra wages could be earned and young and old alike helped to bring in the crops with extra help from gangs of travelling harvesters.

Even so, all work stopped for the photographer to capture two striking poses at Ulehams Farm, Latchingdon (top left) where the Bugg family farmed, and at Dammerwick in Burnham (above) where the bailiff, or 'looker', has a 'guard of honour' before the loaded wagons.

Once the crops were in and the stacks built in the yard, it was left to the thatcher to ensure they were made weather-proof until required for the threshing. These stacks (bottom left) at Marsh House Farm, Tillingham present a sight now lost to us. No longer is there a great need for the straw. The London market for hay and straw required for countless horse-drawn buses, cabs, carriages and wagons had faded away by the 1930s.

Where lan

Before the advent of first rail and then the motor lorry, the obvious way of transporting the produce of the local farms was to make use of the many quays, landing points and marsh outfalls. The flat-bottomed Thames sailing barge was ideally suited for this work, able as it was to load and unload direct from the farms bordering the rivers or sea. Incom-

meets sea

ing cargoes might be loads of Kentish rag-stone for facing the sea walls, or London sewerage farm manure for spreading onto the fields.
Long queues of wagons, waiting to be laboriously unloaded sack by sack, were a common sight after the harvest. Here at Bradwell Quay the s.b. Veronica and s.b. Mayflower are being loaded with grain.

The hay trade

Straw and hay were delivered direct to London's quays as 'stacks' built up on specially rigged barges known as 'stackies'. They were broader in the beam with adjustments to the sails and sprit to accommodate the stack. This early barge (above) with tiller steering is being loaded at Bradwell Quay.

The hay cutter (bottom right) would cut the bales 39 inches long to fit into the barge's width. Here Stevie Gurton and his son Henry, of Tillingham, are pressing the cut hay bales in their home-made press to ensure that each one has the correct weight for a given size. Bales which were destined to be transported by rail were cut shorter to fit the trucks. The Gurtons, like Abe Crosby (top right), also of Tillingham, were thatchers for whom farm work provided the bulk of their freelance work. Sheep shearing was also part of the Gurton's annual round of work.

Steadying the ladder for Abe Crosby is Leslie Attenborough, a Dengie farmer, one of the many northern men who came south to take on successfully the failing Essex farms in the bleak years of the Agricultural Depression, towards the end of the last century.

Steam on the land

Arthur Young's survey of Essex Agriculture in 1806 points to the inventiveness of Dengie farmers and their willingness to try new methods and machinery. Steam power, especially on a contract basis, like this team of Mr. Robinson's at Southminster (above) could cut down on the number of horsemen and their teams, and also bring into cultivation the heavier soils which had previously been left as pasture.

The traction engines worked in pairs pulling the two-way cultivator (left) backwards and forwards between them as they moved along the field headlands. One restricting factor was the need for an adequate nearby water supply to keep the engine steaming. A horse-drawn water cart usually made up the team. At harvest time the engine would provide the power for driving the threshing machine (above). Great care had to be taken to ensure that no hot cinders blew onto the stacks. A stack yard full of closely packed blazing stacks is a fearsome sight!

Windpower

At the beginning of this century Dengie had windmills at Mayland (below), Bradwell (right) and two each at Southminster and Burnham. The last windmill to grind corn was at Southminster; even after its sails were blown off in a gale the stones continued to be turned by a traction engine. The last working mill was the grist mill operated by Mr. Perrin of Tillingham (left) seen here posing beside the Peculiar Peoples' Chapel. He shrewdly built his mill like a three-storey house so its conversion was an easy matter when it ceased to be used as a mill and meal shop.

There were many trades, all locally provided, upon which the farmer depended. There might be two or three smithies in a village, often with an associated wheelwright's shop as in Tillingham (above), where the newly made wooden wheels would be taken to the next door smithy for tyring. (The tyre oven, fixing plate and forges can still be seen today). Carpentry and metalwork on marsh sluices provided extra work for local craftsmen.

Even a small village such as Dengie had its own smithy (below). This one, belonging to Mr. Nunn, and the cottages which stood behind the White Horse, were destroyed by a landmine in the last war.

Supporting services

No less essential to the age of horse and wagon were the products of the harnessmaker and saddler—the harnesses, collars, bits and girths as vital to the life of the community as the motor spares of today. In Tillingham, Charles Hammond (right) would fill the need, acting as village barber when business was slack. Mr. Bull (below) carried on his trade and displayed his ware on Burnham Quay.

Decoy

The thousands of geese and ducks which once flocked to the coast in winter found themselves drawn, willy-nilly, into the marshland economy. In the 17th century, the marshmen adopted a Dutch idea and improved upon it to harvest huge numbers of these duck, providing valuable additional food and income. Indeed, so worthwile a pursuit was this that one man and two dogs could often pay off the farm rents from one season's catch, leaving all the other farm activities to produce clear profit.

No wonder then that the decoys were treated both with secrecy and respect; the decoy took precedence over all other farming activities. Should the wind threaten to carry disturbing noises from nearby workmen, they would be moved forthwith.

Remarkably little effort was required to work the decoy. Leading off a pond were several 'pipes', wire-covered hoops, wide at the pond entrance and tapering down to the catch net. Enticed firstly by grain thrown by the decoyman concealed behind tall reed screens, the ducks were later drawn towards the catch net by the fleeting appearance of the fox-like dogs over the smaller screens. Once they were away from the pond the decoyman would reveal himself behind them. In a panic they rushed into the catch net from which there was no escape.

The pictures are of Marsh House Decoy, one of the last working decoys in Essex. The huge pipe leading in a curve away from the main pond is clearly shown (left). Thomas Tacey, the decoyman, (right) is throwing grain from the basket while his dogs wait expectantly to begin their game of hide and seek over the smaller screens. At the end, Mr. Tacey (below) poses with the tools of his trade and the spoils of the day beside the detachable catch net.

Sporting Dengie

The decline of decoys was attributed to disturbance from the growing use of guns. Wildfowling was both a livelihood and a sport. Walter Linnett (known to many from the books of Wentworth-Day) who lived in the cottage at the edge of the saltings below St Peter's Chapel was well-known and typical of the breed of local wildfowlers.

Whame Moule (left) here outside his cottage in Marsh Road, Tillingham, was another of these wildfowlers-cum-fishermen-cum-longshoremen. He kept his boat and punt in Marsh House Outfall. Even on his sick bed he was known to use his gun, to advantage, through his bedroom window.

This shooting party (bottom) at Dengie used local lads to act as beaters.

Hare coursing was for a long time an organised sport on the marshes. Hares are numerous and unwittingly provided the locals with sport and 'entertainment' throughout the long winter months. The King's Head at Southminster provided both committee room and stopping-off point for the coursers.

Water – too little . .

Water was a crucial factor to the well-being of the marshland village. The shortage that inevitably arose during a hot summer was largely responsible for the high mortality of the marshy coastal areas as the inhabitants resorted to stagnant ponds and polluted rivulets. The problem was a regular cause of concern to the Medical Officer of Health.

It frequently fell to the youngsters' lot to fetch the household water from the local pump, as here at Tillingham (above left) and Bradwell (right). Mobile 'tankers' might be needed for the larger consumers; the barrel on wheels (below) supplied the slaughter house in Marsh Road, Tillingham.

After 1893, Southminster's water supply came from neighbouring Asheldham. Tillingham could have benefited by this scheme but the Parish Council objected on grounds of cost.

The 70-ft high tower was an imposing landmark, overlooking the Iron Age fort in which it stood until its demolition in the late 1950s. Water was extracted from springs rising in the gravel beds, but it has been the extraction of the gravel itself that has shaped present-day Asheldham.

. . . . and too much

On the one hand the problem of drought, on the other the ever-present fear of flood. Constant vigilance was needed to keep the sea from the door. Across the centuries, since sea walls were first built, the need for constant maintenance and occasional heightening has remained. The gradual sinking of the East Coast has created the illusion that tides have been getting higher. Either way, the result has been the same—periodic disaster.

The overflow of 1940 (above) was mildly annoying to the residents of Burnham. The floods of 1897 (right), on the other hand, caused much damage along the Crouch. The water, pouring over the sea-wall (seen top right, just east of the present Royal Corinthian at Burnham), covered acres of farming land and left a wake of destruction in Burnham (bottom right).

PARAFFINE
& COLZA
OILS

The uneasy balance

February 1953 saw our last serious flooding. This area fortunately had no loss of life but livestock were swept away and several thousand acres were resubmerged under salt water. It was all hands to the breaches. Troops were moved in and a WRVS mobile canteen, destined for soldiers working at Bradwell, was skilfully diverted to Marsh House, Tillingham to cater for the local lads fighting to mend a breach with endless sandbags (above).

Land, once reclaimed from the sea, can so easily be won back by the sea. Around the Dengie coast several hundred acres of once fertile land have since been abandoned. After two successive floods, Bridgemarsh Island at Althorne was finally left in 1930 to the wild-fowl. The last occupants, the Gooch's, had lived in the upper rooms of the farm house optimistically hoping for the island's recovery. The precarious lifestyle of Dengie, rugged and individualistic, is still to this day as close to the surface as the sea is to its door.

ACKNOWLEDGEMENTS

The photographs in this book are drawn from the collections of the Burnham and District Local History and Amenity Society and of the Editor. Between them the two collections cover the whole range of facets of the life of the Dengie peninsula and they grow steadily more comprehensive as new additions are made to them.

The collections—and, therefore, this booklet—have been made possible only by the generous willingness of so many people to share with others the pleasure and significance of their treasured photographic mementoes. To all of them, whether their contribution has been by way of a single item or a whole album, I would offer my thanks. Special thanks are also due to those members of the Society who have so patiently assisted in the preparation of this work.

The map of Dengie is reproduced with the sanction of The Controller of H.M.S.O. Items on pages 18 and 33 appear by courtesy of N. Sharp and D. Lambert respectively.

Kevin Bruce
June 1981

FURTHER READING

Benham, Hervey — *Last stronghold of sail,* 1948

Day, J. Wentworth — *Coastal adventure,* 1949

Gramolt, D.W. — 'Coastal marshlands of East Essex between the 17th and mid-19th centuries' (unpublished M.A. Thesis, University of London, 1960; copy in Essex Record Office)

Grieve, Hilda — *The Great Tide,* 1959

Essex Landscape No.1: historic features. E.C.C. Planning Dept., 2nd edn.1979